ERASABLE
WALLS

The New Issues Press Poetry Series

Editor	Herbert Scott
Advisory Editors	Nancy Eimers, Mark Halliday William Olsen, J. Allyn Rosser
Assistant to the Editor	Rebecca Beech
Assistant Editors	Allegra Blake, Jenny Burkholder, Becky Cooper, Rita Howe Scheiss, Nancy Hall James, Kathleen McGookey, Tony Spicer
Editorial Assistants	Melanie Finlay, Pamela McComas
Business Manager	Michele McLaughlin
Fiscal Officer	Marilyn Rowe

The New Issues Press Poetry Series is sponsored by The College of Arts and Sciences, Western Michigan University.

First Edition, 1998.

ISBN: 0-932826-59-8 (cloth)
ISBN: 0-932826-60-1 (paper)

Library of Congress Cataloging-in-Publication Data:
Larsen, Lance, 1961–
Erasable Walls / Lance Larsen
Library of Congress Catalog Card Number (97-069531)

Art Direction:	Tricia Hennessy
Design:	Cun W. Sulestio
Production:	Paul Sizer
	The Design Center, Department of Art
	College of Fine Arts
	Western Michigan University
Printing:	Bookcrafters, Chelsea, Michigan

ERASABLE WALLS

LANCE LARSEN

FOREWORD BY RICHARD HOWARD

New Issues Press

WESTERN MICHIGAN UNIVERSITY

For Jacqui

*I have perceived that in all cases man must eventually
lower, or at least shift, his conceit of attainable felicity;
not placing it anywhere in the intellect or the fancy;
but in the wife, the heart, the bed, the table, the saddle,
the fire-side, the country.*

Herman Melville, *Moby-Dick*

Contents

III

Foreword

"What Might Pass as Play": Lance Larsen's *Erasable Walls*

He may have a more recondite accounting for his title than the one
I should like to propose, for on the evidence of these poems Larsen is a man
who holds his cards very close to the chest, inward, downward, anything but
toward the *opposite player*. I'd wager, though, or warrant that the walls can be
erased by their very consistency as poems, as structures of language which dis-
solve barriers. Even certain doctrinal practices, certain rituals are seen, here,
as soluble obstructions, and it is the intimacies, the secrets of the Larsen poem
which spirit away confines. A characteristic action is one of release, apparent
destruction and loss which eventuate in ecstatic illumination.

He leads us in rather gently. The earlier poems appear to concern,
indeed to construct, what we so often call, with a grimace of wrong recogni-
tion, *family values*. How disingenuously the poet's persona muses upon the
responsibilities of fatherhood, of filial piety, of those initiations into man's
estate which involve certain severances, certain deliberate repudiations. And
how clearly he speaks an American idiom it is his special rhythm to celebrate:

> . . . my mother in a whatever
> shade of lipstick was holding a dead cat
> wrapped in Visqueen. She had errands
> to run, and Dead Pet Hill was on the way.
> I dug, she watched. Deep lipstick, suggesting
> what—aloofness and downtown commerce?
> Or maybe a lighter shade, to go with
> the inside-out smell of rain and too much
> sagebrush. I don't know the color.
> But wet looking and waxy and a favorite
> kind of candy all at once

These lines sound the purest native note I've heard in our new poetry. Even
Ashbery, invoked in a later poem, occasionally rings a little exotic compared to
or collated with "Dead Pet hill was on the way. / I dug, she watched." And it is
by means of these apparent saliences that the poet moves us away from what
Melville—in a phrase Larsen takes as his shocking epigraph—calls "attainable
felicities" to be located not "in the intellect or the fancy; but in the wife, the
heart, the bed, the table, the saddle, the fire-side, the country." The poet moves
us away from the known, the approved, the predictable and into strange terrain
indeed. By the second half of this handsome and so insistently homemade

book of poems, the walls have indeed been erased, and we are at a contact high:

> . . . if the only way
> to keep the urn alive is by calling it bride,
> why not? Besides, there's freedom in seeing your gods
> dissolve like clouds. Ask Stevens. It gives you
> back yourself.

Again and again Larsen works his modest (but pervasive) wonder, he reaches transport, rapture, aloft by what he likes to call, in poetry, "mostly device", though it is rather more inspired than that. I suspect the ascent is achieved by staying so close to what we might call intra-terrestrial visits. The walls can be most readily erased, then, by the predications of death, or at least of dying. We are moved into a solitude—a religious solitude, if there are kinds—best represented by these last lines from "A Philanthropist Speaks to His Lawyer", lines among the grandest American diction since the Stevens Larsen has evidently "asked":

> . . . drop me into a hole
> with the indigents—my bones, their bones.
> It's enough if hyacinths mark us. Or a fig
> tree, so that if I rise, I will first smell
> heavy sweetness. A sullen morning it will be,
> birds slower, toads dreaming in the ferns.
> I'm tired. I feel it most in the afternoons.

The walls are gone, we are in the clear, in what another of Larsen's forbears calls the Radiance. And happy to be there.

Richard Howard

Acknowledgments

Boulevard: "Young Woman to Her Husband"
Fine Madness: "Black Sand"
Gulf Coast: "Cityscape"
Hudson Review: "February 1922: My Father's Conception"
Kenyon Review: "Peach"
The Literary Review: "Against Cosmology"
New Republic: "Walking Around"
Paris Review: "Interview," "Nest"
Poetry East: "A Missionary Considers His Converts"
Poetry Wales: "Dreaming Yourself Pregnant," "A Philanthropist
    Speaks to His Lawyer"
Quarterly West: "Errand," "Fisherman Rant," "Grande Valse
    Brillante," "Lips"
Salmagundi: "And Also Much Cattle," "Interiors,"
    "Funeral Home," "Rhetoric Summer"
Shenandoah: "Driving I-70," "Elegy for Donald Pugmire,
    Photographer"
Tar River Poetry: "Desire," "Solstice"
Weber Studies: "Woman Addressing the Moon"
Western Humanities Review: "Bath House Overlooking Family
    Cemetery," "Denouement"
Wisconsin Review: "Smoke"
Writers at Work 1994: "Throwing Papers"

I would like to thank Richard Howard, Susan Elizabeth Howe,
Timothy Liu, and Leslie Norris for their friendship and support;
and Chase Twichell for her support of this manuscript. I am
indebted to the Cultural Arts Council of Houston and the Utah
Arts Council for grants that made this collection possible.

February 1922: My Father's Conception

Leona, Ershel—names chalked on someone's driveway,
names mapping the erasable walls of the heart.
Paired in loopy cursive, they were supposed to fade,
like memory, like the light from the open doorway
of the Elks' lodge after a Saturday night dance,
couples fanning out across the rutted road.

Certainly, no one was thinking of weddings.
Not Leona, not Ershel. Not the town drunk
who saluted all young lovers, with sincerity
and a bottle from the upriver bridge. Not
the German baker working late, who would one day
offer Ershel a life of ovens and floury hands.

Least of all their Mormon bishop, aged walrus,
snoring now beside his flanneled, pliant wife.
And if it was that night, where did they end up—
Leona's basement, a barn loft? Or maybe
a bunkhouse closed for the winter, the wind
and the rustling of dusty blankets

shuttering them in, as my grandfather,
sad country boxer, clenched his eyes against
this new pleasure, fevered colors swimming
through his head, while my grandmother
whispered to the wall, if I hurry, if I hurry,
if I hurry and wash up with vinegar.

Dreaming Yourself Pregnant

Asleep beside me, you dream of babies,
a gleaming pail of them you stir
with your finger. Or inside you,
slippery warm, three or four swimming
slow circles like tadpoles. I watch
the walls and think of a girl I hugged
at sock hops, pigeon chested, safe
as a brother. That October the girls
watched a film. We knew. The quiet one,
Armenian, hair all spirals and dips—
she started first. It was almost Christmas.
Bleeding as if she'd cut off a finger.
By lunch, everyone knew. *Asya*—it was
a conjured name, her body a new kind
of weather. We were sailors, vigilant
and afraid. As for that girl I hugged—
no rain in her voice, no damp countries.
Hugging her was like hugging myself,
like touching a flower I hoped would
never open. When I touched older girls,
rooms unclenched and I fell through them.
With you, it is the same. I kiss you
awake, you pin me against shadows.
Still there's too much skin between us.
You, she, I, they . . . Knowing, not
knowing. And now a touch: how you
explain your dreams, how you refuse.
They hang here—scratchy whispers
in a foreign movie, the same phrase
over and over, pleasurable tiny stabs.

Desire

A kind of infidelity—walking these streets alone.
Your salt on my tongue, but me watching
neighborhood houses balloon with invisible

heat. Old men feel it pirouetting in the margins
of rattled newspapers. Children cry out,
seeing it gleam on unwashed windows.

And lovers, coaxing it from fluted walls,
wear it for the moment—a glitter that makes
an electrical map of their bodies.

But it escapes them, as it escapes us all—
to condense on banisters, on ripening fruit
and goblet rims, on coats closeted against

summer's heat. Tonight it gathers in the hung
darkness of backyard gazebos. Wells up,
then surges on the distant chords of Rachmaninoff.

Part crescendo, part fiery ache, which I follow
to the corner. In a lit window, a girl
with braided hair leans into a baby grand.

Behind her, a second girl touches her shoulder.
The room fills with what they cannot name,
keys glowing like an oiled back, and the hands

attack again, in what might pass as play.

Grande Valse Brillante

Not the arpeggios from our garage-sale upright,
or my wife's wrists lifting, but a bathrobed neighbor
leaning from his zinnias. That's what woke me
up to myself, a bear of a man sniffing the air
for Chopin. It makes me want to try my cheesiest
waltz step, to hug that uncombed, barefooted
grizzly and romp straight into the heat. Maybe
the grace notes lifted him back fifteen years—
an afternoon when his wife, pretending to check
food storage, led him to the cool basement
then kissed her way from deep winter to August
harvest. And afterwards? A dicey minuet
among rows of pickled beets. *Grande Valse Brillante*—
to say it is to run your tongue along a halved
peach. To hear it is to believe small disturbances
sometimes chart the sublime. My son for instance
in a nest of unfolded laundry—arching his back
to deliver a clutch of onyx eggs. What matters
is his toes think they're tadpoles, my chin
is bumping out rhythm, and I'm ready for once
to celebrate. Camisoles, ferns, how-to books,
artichoke salad, humidity—everything. My wife
has a migrating birthmark I haven't kissed
in months. Sometimes the timbre of dying
eighth notes is so much like applause or a burst
of rain I keep checking to see if it's my shadow
or me or the rest of the room that is rising.

A Place Like That

Early summer, 1922, and the boxer and WWI vet
I will one day call grandfather has rolled off
Leona weeks ago. Just her in this Iowa field,
and me floating above, voyeur and incidental
relative. I've brought my father along, growing
inside her, so we'll have two pairs of eyes.

Make us owls coursing, and her a dimple
in this confusion of green. Make her nineteen,
though in her wedding portrait, which a half-mute
Czech will sketch inside the family bible,
she looks more niece than bride. Let her
pretend this thumb of a baby is an offering

the prairie will take back if only she lies
still enough. She closes her eyes, and the waving
of grass passes around, then through her. A sign?
And her breathing, calm finally, like sleep
laced with church hymns—call that another.
She swallows slowly, and erases his fingers,

his mouth, finally his hips. If she rolls
to her stomach, she can bury his boy laugh,
the stubby cigarettes, and the ice in his eyes
when he bragged of killing Germans in the trenches.
Twilight, and we settle in a tree, my father
and I, which affords a view of her walking away.

Leona carrying her first, and only, child.
All around her the darkening grass ripples,
but not like an ocean. Chancier—as if
buffalo lived just under the prairie's skin.
On windy nights, she can feel the grass
sharpening its roots on those terrible shoulders.

Inventing Leona

Lean my head into a sour flank, let shit
splash up around my ankles. I'm getting
it wrong, my grandmother's life, mistaking
bone-cold winter for epic, a pitchfork
through the foot and chilblains for understanding.
I'm also proving I can't milk a cow.

Iowa, Iowa, Iowa. Saying it slowly, as she did,
like a pledge or prayer. Swallowing it too,
the way her father, drunk and tied to a captain's
chair, swallowed mashed apples the morning
after they pulled his molars. And I'm trying
not to forget her mother's goiter—which filled

every room, or floated at eye level, a talisman,
a crystal ball I might have rubbed for glimpses
of my uncertain future. But Leona, she's lost
in a hand mirror someone's hidden in a drawer.
Her bird laugh, the cheap floral of her dresses—
that's all I can conjure. I can bring back

Eddie, her only brother, who shot off his ear
(or was it a neighbor's?) on Thanksgiving
and compiled a Book of the Dead out of wrinkled
funeral programs and a pair of cigar box lids.
But Leona? She's the tightening of a room
you've walked away from, or if you held her,

the smell of skin and apology. To make attribution
easier, I'm giving her two sisters instead
of five. The one who moved to Des Moines
and was killed by a runaway buggy. And the other—
who bottled her wedding ring in a pint of pears.
I can even make out the tornado when she was seven,

but not Leona herself. Just her button-eyed
doll with the unstitched foot, and when
the house lifted above her, a row of summer hams
swinging from the floorboards. Which means
I'm left to consider the cow she milked—
smelly, holding her milk back, like this cow

I've just given up on. Morning and evening,
my grandmother holding the same swollen udder.
Duchess, the nickname she went by as a girl.
Why the hell Duchess? No one can tell me.
She leans into that sour flank, the moos
growing louder, like anger or passionate talk.

Black Sand

Sometimes when I'm walking
into a morning I can't explain,
I think of Yosef Karsh, how
in his portraits, he reduces
personality to pattern—tangled
swatches of gray and white.
And sometimes when I touch
my wife or hear her voice
ticking through a thunderstorm
toward a drugstore pay phone
in Laramie, which I feed
with quarters and call my own,
I imagine hanging that moment,
or a cluster of moments,
in a gallery downtown, frozen
like boot prints in damp ground.
In time the pictures dissolve,
except for a grainy five-by-seven
I hadn't thought of showing—
my wife kneeling beside our bed,
my face in the mirror, floor boards
between us glowing like black sand.
Then one afternoon at closing,
a stranger stops by, studies
the way the shadows lean and bleed,
and asks himself, in a voice
that makes me believe answers
matter, *Why is she praying?*
and what will happen next?

Solstice

Quiet enough for evening to begin its apologies.
A sullen cough of cicadas and backfiring cars.
Then wind, with its slow fingers, plinking

the aspens. A bedroom light flicks on, another.
In the compost heap, a sliced iris bulb
bearing my signature listens for lost colors.

An unlit street lamp, children assembling for tag.
They scuffle and bend. They carry whole
streets on an extended finger. Behind them,

a tipped lemonade stand. To touch and be touched.
Sometimes a dollar a glass, sometimes free.
Behind them, a moon looking nothing like a face.

Lips

Our cars were used and named after singers,
our cats always Siamese and dying.
Which fails as zen or science, but helps
explain why Ethel, our '58 Fairlane,
was stalled on a muddy road overlooking
Pocatello, and why my mother in a whatever
shade of lipstick was holding a dead cat
wrapped in Visqueen. She had errands
to run, and Dead Pet Hill was on the way.
I dug, she watched. Deep lipstick, suggesting
what—aloofness and downtown commerce?
Or maybe a lighter shade, to go with
the inside-out smell of rain and too much
sage brush. I don't know the color.
But wet looking and waxy and a favorite
kind of candy all at once. She dabbed
her mouth with her hanky. It was April first,
her birthday. Which meant blue omelets
for breakfast, and later that night, noodles
and the whole fam-damily at the Shanghai.
But for now just me, my mother turning 47,
and a cat to bury. Easy digging, on account
of the rain and I'd already done my crying
over the weekend. Except for a few roots
and chopped worms, the sides chiseled
clean, as if I were uncovering a hole
already there. Her mouth was smeared.
Nothing like her practice lips—blotted
on a pane of tissue each morning and floating
wet and flat before she flushed them.
That impeccable smile. She was waiting
for me. We had the car to start, then errands.
Bakery, library, the florist, a utilities bill . . .
Me running the easy ones, the car idling

and warm. I wanted to save all that, and her.
The hole deep enough but making it deeper,
bending sometimes to touch the clean sides.

Red

Because it might hurt, and because looseness
in a baby tooth, especially an eye tooth
bleeding a little, is its own virtue, my son

refuses to let me pull it, though he's happy
to let it bleed slowly and exquisitely
onto the unbuttered roll he holds to his mouth,

so that a tiny blossom forms, which he bites off
and chews, all the time staring at the ceiling light
and counting breaths or ghosts or dead moths maybe,

until his chewing gathers this quiet into a kind
of questioning, which makes me think of Jacqui
waking in Recovery after her first miscarriage

and the possum-faced nurse who brought in a tray
of cherry Jell-o and cranberry juice, and said,
Eat up, Sister, eat up, as if it was color

she had lost, and Jacqui laughed, and I lay
down beside her and I laughed, and she gulped
the juice, then started in on the Jell-o, but slowly,

taking tiny bites to make it last, this red,
like my son eating blood in the kitchen's murky
half-darkness, and me watching, half hungry.

Walking Around

Sometimes it's loss I want, a slow acid eating
my bones, wife and son gone forever,
loss that would color this moon a sad yellow
and give these houses voices beneath their paint.

I would sleep by day, and my grief,
the thinnest of shirts, would hide me
from nothing. At night: the shrieks of birds,
my wife's heart thrumming in the trunks

of the thickest trees, my son buried
somewhere or falling asleep to voices he's never
heard, pajamas white as baby teeth,
the birthmark under his chin a closed flower.

And maybe before following the night's meanders,
I would glance up at these windows furred
by porch light and frost, where my wife
and son are sleeping now, and try to invent

the darkness where we dream, the three of us,
like plants bedded in a window-box, so intertwined
we no longer hear the song of our leaves,
or feel the tangle and sprawl of our roots.

Fisherman Rant

Stupid, the way I'm lobbing this plastic
    bubble and fly, a Royal Coachman if names matter,
        into a smelly river so my six-year-old can lure
            fish we don't want from under a falling-down bridge,

and stupid how mad it makes me, not mosquitoes
    or mud up to my ankles, not even yesterday's
        fish guts staring at me from the grass like an inkblot
            test in lies, till dipping, and treason from some past life—

but the river itself, private and moving
    and vaginal: I mean the way it buries all questions
        in eddies and silt, then hints that I'm betraying
            myself, or something grand and impossible, with each cast,

or maybe it's time I'm betraying, since my father
    tied this fly in 1968, over a dry salami sandwich
        on his lunch hour at FMC, using not peacock herl as you're
            supposed to but a tuft of reddish seven-year-old boy hair,

my hair, and shouldn't there be a statute
    of limitations, since how long can you trust
        the savvy of a geologist-father who paid Tony the Barber
            in dimes for his son's bowl cut, then swept up the curls

into an outdated *Field and Stream*, as if a fly's
    color didn't matter then, though of course it did,
        and does, since this is the exact fly these know-nothing
            chubs are taking, even if it is too hot and my son keeps

crying about peeing his pants during
    the hike in, which is stupid since the fish
        can't see him, so I tell him so, *and even if they could,*
            I say, *they swim in piss and worse, and besides your pants*

will dry and everyone pees himself
    sometimes, even your mom, and I cast again
        into what must be a tavern of chubs, a whole
            drooling masonic lodge full of them, not with a cane rod

and tapered line like my father used,
    but with a cracked float and a cast-it-clear-
        the-hell-out-there, garage-sale reel, which plonks
            like a bad Hail Mary pass, and my son reels in, screaming,

German brown, German brown, like this
    was salvation, though in fact it's just east Wyoming
        off I-80, and another chub, which will make nine I've
            clubbed and tossed into the brush, and the swallows

just make it worse, the way they thread
    the creosote trestles, trailing pieces of god
        behind them but stitching closed any pockets of sky
            that might explain this moment, or my left-hander's

bad luck, or why my father, who can't drive
    anymore, won't just give me his rods and Medalist
        reels, and why I keep worrying about coming back
            as a fish or caddis fly or a six-year-old, since I'd prefer

not to come back at all, which is why
    I hate Saturday mornings and their nothing promises
        of renewal, and if I had a bottle of crusty salmon eggs
            I'd pop seven or eight into my mouth—they're not poison

like everyone says—and squeeze them
    behind my eye teeth and suck down that briny
        taste of death and say to hell with the grace
            of these swallows doing their bird thing so well.

II

Errand

Not God dissolving in a coin of gluten,
but how bread tastes—that miracle.
Your errand, tongue, to know
the exact savor of the world's flesh.
Then to translate beyond it.
Yours to gather this fragmented body.
Tireless epicurean, winebibber,
connoisseur of bile and perfumed skin:
teach us the delicacy of manna.
What nourishes. What sometimes
rots. How even worms prepare us.

Letter to Hieronymus Bosch

It's June, friend, which means I'm staring at a detail
from the second panel of your *Garden of Earthly
Delights*. Tacky, having you monthed and hanging
on my fridge—but also sublime. April equals the Fall.
October, Apocalypse. In between, the greens and blues
of this world and a chance to test the ends of nakedness.

I'm Eve in a floating apple. No, I'm Adam holding
a cluster of berries the size of a side of beef.
Or make me one of the hungry sods, leaning
with his mouth. Beguiling, this landscape, Hieronymus,
but like your upside-down man, buried to his ribs
in pond, I need more than a pair of hands to hide

my nakedness. Besides, I can't tell the damned
from the redeemed. Is that your intent—everyone
suffering the same numbed-out bliss? If only God
could fill us with knowledge, or lock our genitals
away inside the family bible. If only I hadn't peeked
ahead to October—bodies burned, drowned, skewered.

This afternoon I found a mouse with a chewed-off head
on my doorstep. What was he guilty of? If tossing
him into the field was a kind of prayer, I offered it
quickly, but didn't mean it. A single, lazy arc.
Later, I washed my hands, checked the calendar,
and headed for the jacuzzi. Which I did mean.

June, month of my parents' thirty-second anniversary
but no holidays. And this coming week? Bills
to pay, potato salad for our C-sectioned neighbor,
a root canal. And my wife four more days in Syracuse.
No surprise, then, that your lovers inside a giant
clam are what I carry from the calendar into the water.

True, I don't know they're lovers. All I can see
are three legs and part of a hand. And it's hard
to tell about the hand. Is it prying the shell open?
Holding on for better leverage? Then there's
the stooped guy balancing it all on his back—
how long his day, how long this burden of limbs?

Young Woman to Her Husband

They didn't make me sad, the hymns.
It was May, and there was whiteness
to consider—how it pooled on the tiled
walls of the rest room. Not God
on our tongues, but the dispenser
holding open its mouth for a quarter.
Its enamel gave us back ourselves
in scratches, three combed girls.
My face, sunburned. My dress blue
or maybe yellow with blue pockets.
The dress doesn't matter, except to say
it was cotton, with a skin smell
to it, a tartness. Who can say
whose quarter, whose hand? We all
reached. It could have been a Vegas
slot machine the way we reached.
I wasn't thinking of some boy Adonis
on top of me or children unfurling
like pop-up dolls. But the waiting—
it was just like that. And then
we had the napkin, thin and white.
No bigger than a doll house mattress.
And we were outside, beyond the hedges,
lilac so thick it purpled the air.
We knelt. Dug with our fingers. Making
the hole clean like the graves you dig
for dead mice. One girl had a pen.
We signed the napkin in leaning red
cursive. Then came the initials,
the boy you happened to like—his initials.
I signed D.P. for my brother's friend
with the shriveled ear who could walk
across our porch, whistling, on his hands.
But I was thinking D.P.—that could

be anyone. We passed the napkin
around and smelled it, its whiteness.
We didn't kiss it, though I wanted to.
Then we buried it, and the church bell
began tolling, and we hurried off
to our parents' hot cars and their questions
about what it meant to believe.

Woman Addressing the Moon

I want to sing without God
burning in my mouth.

Or sit in a perfumed bath
and feel oceans lapping inside me.

I want to pass fruit vendors,
with their sharp elbows and crooked beards,
and not see lust staining their eyes.

I will dress myself in white linen.

My kisses to the air will bring rain.
Will erase ministers who smile
with their neckties.

I will return to a country
green with fountains and tree frogs
where I believed I was pure

and I was.

Interview

A problem *muy adentro*, she tells him, deep
inside her—a metal loop like a piece
of Satan, but the doctor who was supposed
to remove it on vacation. All the while
her hands churning at her belt line
like paddle wheels. To this, add crying.
And now her question: Can God make her
clean with this coiled thing still inside?

This the baptismal interview, this
the gringo missionary's first confession
from a girl his age. Between them,
a scratch on her mother's kitchen table.
A paring knife and sliced pomegranate.
Is it him, or the room? Some sort of pulsing.
He does not want to picture the loop.
Or watch the hands churning. He wants
to build a church for her out of words,
invite her to pass inside. Instead,
wounds splay the walls, her closed-eyed
lovers squirming the table. He keeps
his eyes moving. When he speaks—his voice,
but inside him a burning like a flock
of birds. *Renewal, font, Jesus—*
words that hover, then pass between them.
They seem inside out and too small.

He opens his book to a clean page. Writes
her name and birth date. Then her city,
which he keeps spelling wrong. *La Cisterna*,
she says. Cistern. Like this—a vessel,
a place of water. She makes a pitcher
out of air, and for an instant, the room
gathers at her fingers. She holds

before him what nestles inside her.
He has crossed some barrier, he knows,
this boy who in nineteen years has been
with no one but himself. He is saying
what sounds like God's name. Asking
for something. Darkness maybe. Or blood.
He knows it has to do with thirst.

A Missionary Considers His Converts

For weeks, we did nothing but walk
dirt roads and shake hands, saying hello.
We carried bricks for old women, hoed gardens,
put on puppet shows, made five-peso coins
sprout like corn from their children's ears.
Finally, they began opening their doors.

The first was a half-blind cobbler, who gave
us *yerba maté* in heavy mugs, called us sons.
We've taught *campesinos*, store keepers,
the mayor, his three cloistered sisters,
even his mother, who owns the bar and half the town.
And we've baptized twenty-three.

We help them to believe in God, not images,
then we ask for their statues, their false books.
Today, after just three visits, we walked away
heavy as pack horses, unloading everything
in our backyard along the fence—Saints and angels,
wooden Madonnas, a crucifix worn brown by kisses.

Looking out at the clutter, Elder Hansen started
to laugh. Three months out, but already happy
in this work, teachable, never imagining a world
without God. Why not burn it? he said.
And I nodded, imagining statues melting in smoke,
the whole superstitious mess dumped

into a shallow grave beneath our window.
But tonight, awake suddenly, my belief
a borrowed shirt too long in the sleeves,
I feel like saving them. Above me, cold stars.
While here, along the fence, washed in moonlight,
smile gods I can hold in my hand.

A Philanthropist Speaks to His Lawyer

I don't mind giving it away—the estate,
the refineries, the beach front in Bermuda,
my Shakespeare folios and Rothko rectangles.
Stipulate that no one touch my organs.
When my heart gives, pack me in dry ice
and ship me south—Lima or Santiago.
Hire a driver, pay him twice what he asks.
Drive until you find a hobbling woman
with veined calves. If she turns down a lane
thick with squealing pigs, if her house
puts on a scrubbed glow when she opens
the gate, follow her to the door. Check
for sadness braiding her hair, evenings
pressed into her heavy skirt, then ask her
to bury me. Tell her I'm a vagrant or amnesiac,
anything. Humming softly, she will rub me
with scented oils, then lay me between
her sofa and a broken radio. Children
will feel my blood pooling in the rain.
For three days let mourners kiss the glass
over my face, then drop me into a hole
with the indigents—my bones, their bones.
It's enough if hyacinths mark us. Or a fig
tree, so that if I rise, I will first smell
heavy sweetness. A sullen morning it will be,
birds slower, toads dreaming in the ferns.
I'm tired. I feel it most in the afternoons.

Rhetoric Summer

I used to be an organicist, Coleridgean
to the core—content and form as one fiber.
Forget the rigid silk box you untie for a nugget
of truth. Poetry was the thing itself: egg,
apple, black-eyed Susan. The point was—
keep it natural. A homegrown cabbage would do.
The sap of God blessing even the blemishes.

Detox time. I fell back on my first gift,
weak-minded doggedness. Eight hours a day,
weekends off, a break every hour to take a leak.
I started at 467 BC and ended with Derrida
and friends. One by one, they trooped across
my mind's stage, pausing to curtsy or belch
or lecture, and I watched, bending their dogma

into elaborate pictographs I could memorize.
Plato was plate. Socrates, a pair of argyle socks.
Figure of thought—my wife's figure plushly pink,
a light bulb of thought balanced on her forehead.
I scanned these peep shows forward, backward
until they felt like family movies: Cicero
and Aunt Mimi and me doing the Roman courts.

Augustine, I admit, was my favorite—traitor
to both Greek and Christian. He turned Aristotle
on his head, made *ethos* real virtue, not the kind
you project like a good baritone. At the same time,
he bedded down with rhetoric, chasing his gift
like a sodomite after fleeing angels. So—
a bundle of contradictions. But what a preacher.

Still there's the fig tree episode to figure out:
Take up and read, take up and read. That voice—

ventriloquism, or godly mystery? And what about
poetry in general? The spontaneous overflow,
dear William tells us. But rhetoric flows as easily
as feeling. Who can say who's pulling the strings?
This much I know—it's done with hexes and grace.

And if poetry is mostly device, if the only way
to keep the urn alive is by calling it bride,
why not? Besides, there's freedom in seeing your gods
dissolve like clouds. Ask Stevens. It gives you
back yourself. As for the voice Augustine heard—
don't forget the sing-song rhythm, the sleepy
shade of the tree—who wouldn't have followed?

And Also Much Cattle

What did they look like—those cows God
took notice of in sparing Nineveh?
Bland-faced no doubt, eyes big as chestnuts.
Jonah must have loathed them. Jonah under
the gourd, Jonah in his cobbled-together
martyr's booth, sulking and praying
for plagues. Anything to teach Nineveh
a lesson. If not a cracked sky drumming
fire, then leprosy, or wells curdled
with blood. As for the cows, if Jonah
followed their grazing too long, he must
have pictured them fasting again—tricked
out in sackcloth, ashes brindling their sides.
Such cheap theatrics. Didn't real penitence
mean casting yourself into God's mouth,
and waking in the nave of His bowels?
Just you and an acidy soup of sin and rotting
fish. Those three days, they should have
clinched it for him—God's golden boy.
Now Jonah wondered. He tried shutting
his eyes, tried, but the drove wouldn't slow.
All those hooves and splattered flanks.
Cows whose only offering was a little snot
on the muzzle, maybe a cracked tongue.
Cows milling until their moos echoed
across the fatness of the afternoon
like untuned pleas deep inside a fish.

Denouement

As for Adam, his labor was to name,
so he strolled, strange forked animal,
scattering syllables the way farmers
sow seeds, but with a magician's exactness.
When he said *birch*, a papery skin of stillness
hugged the trunk, then rustled along bent
branches. When he said *raccoon*, the name
settled like dew upon the creature's face,
a blessing that only later became a mask.
No puns, or panting *double-entendres*.
And no punctuation—all commas and periods
swallowed by a grammar of infinity:
for who can parse God? Adam's troubles
began when he tackled the possessive:
Bone of my bones, and flesh of my flesh . . .
Think of his voice—thunderous, priestly,
veiling the earth in a cascade of darkness.
Anything, I suppose, to ease the throb
of his missing rib. But what could *one flesh*
mean to Eve?—who believed the breath
of life was a gift, and herself already whole.

Letter from Longitude X

Dear Giselle,
Borders in dispute, and no sign of the Milky Way.
Which has meant luna moths and paranormal
eavesdropping among the peasants. Send no pictures.
As the Colonel says, faces are the first thing
you lose out here. For now, the Carolina slant
of your cursive is enough. I have you raucously

pretty and at obtuse angles. I have you pale
as a parson's wife. (And on lucky nights, at every station
of the cross in between.) The quartermaster calls
you a prank, an apparitional projection beamed back
at me from a broken satellite. What about her pink
ink on green paper? I say. Or the way she stars

her i's? To prove him wrong, Giselle, use only
pet names, send fingernail parings, repeat what
my birthmark reminds you of. There's less and less
of me. Weighed against what I remember of drive-ins,
pennies, all things stupid and American, I'm no more
than swamp fog, the acidy stuff we paddle through

on patrol. I feel scraps of myself drifting off toward
corpses in the maples. Lucky then how this longitude burns
my longings holy. After chewing the ink from your letters,
I offer them to a local saint—a pulpy ball between
the knuckles of his first and second toes. Protection
for me, good harvest for the paraplegic fisherman I buy

black tea and lighters from in the next village.
If I close my eyes at midday, the skin over your ribs
sharpens the whole landscape, foot bridges included.
I say your eyebrows and wrists like prayer. I drink

water I pretend has passed though you, until even
the turkey vultures roosting in the cathedral wear skins

of charity. Giselle, the tarantulas are bigger than usual,
and striped. If you are other than who your letters
claim, meeting in Marrakesh or Budapest is definitely off.
I'm thinking of you in cipher and with every curled
hair. Kiss your sister's baby for me. Anybody's
baby. If you see a nun walking, offer her a ride.

She

After John Ashbery

She owns a freshly dunged garden and knows what to bury
    there.
She, with those teeth and ankles.
She leans stiffly into the wind, pure hypotenuse, and
    mathematicians measure her backbone.
She only sometimes wears socks.

She before spring run off, after the invention of peaches.
She, babysitting late, sneaks a look into the reproduction
    drawer.
She prefers to sleep in a house made of cards.
She is only rarely a noun.

She prefers that the cards face in and show royalty in doric
    undergarments.
She bathes the twins in a tub floating with blue dinosaurs.
She whispers *Eve* at every celebration, including volcanoes,
    because it is spelled the same backwards.
She invents an alphabet out of longing and Malaysian
    postage stamps.

She, with shaved head, during lap swim, counting tiles and
    difficult half-truths.
She warms her Christmas bed with a borrowed blow dryer.
She recognizes in a dying fig tree at dawn an exact
    mistranslation of sadness.
She is the Ur text, the last remaindered copy.

She forwards all prayers and W2s straight to Lesbos, or is it
    Patmos?
She, he said, I'm telling you, she and no one else, she she she.
She smuggles in dualities with the cilantro.

She considers Sunday mornings and a mound of white irises
    sufficient.

She remains highly theoretical.
She is the laminated bookmark moved from *Ecclesiastes*, to
    The Prince, to *Architectural Digest*.
She tunes the Celestial Top 40 by rubbing her navel.
She prefers broken kore figures to conceptual art.

She he she he she he she.
She can't make up her mind between Elvis and Mozart.
She on a Cleveland park bench reading Nietzsche but preferring
    jicama and crows.
She no longer believes in blood sacrifice.

She, lost in the poem in the spirit in the flesh.
She organizes our best thoughts like a Bolivian peasant carding
    wool.
She winks sometimes from tall buildings.
She signs herself Sor Juana, Simone, Joan of, Billie, whatever.

She has a flotilla of moles that may hasten world peace.
She riffles history for *trompe l'oeil* pleasures that might work at
    this late hour.
She uses croquet mallets and lipstick as a last resort, and only
    if promises were made.
She will not be leaving any time soon.

Nest

The things I saved up there—mantis legs, cat fur,
porcupine quills tied with twine. I thought
this was religion. To climb through leaves

and pocked apples to the highest bough, to finger
what no one else wanted. Cicada husk,
dried fish tail. Not death, but what it left

behind. I touched tongue to rabbit skull, tasted
the eye holes. So many creeds, and only a crooked
wind and the sulfur glow of the railroad yards

to help do the sorting. Snake skin wrapping
my knuckles, the clink of wisdom teeth, my aunt's.
Worn down enough to make me think of food.

What it might mean to chew. And be chewed.
That divination. Then putting everything
back. Bone puzzle, flesh pieced against fur.

And swallowing as I climbed down—the creature
above and inside me now. Anything left over
circling like a hawk or unanswered prayer.

Funeral Home

Lungs—you could smell them.
He held them like bloated fish,
a big, slithery one leaking brown juice,
the other one puffy and clean and pink.
The good one is Mrs. Daley,
he said, *eighty-four years old.*
This other guy—over two packs
a day, and not even forty.
To his left, scalpels fanned out
like silverware. Behind him,
a power drill with industrial bits.
Even then I knew this was not
about careers. But who cared?
He was explaining the slow dissolve
of the body, how it unlocks
itself to the blade. At the room's
center, a dented steel table
and tubes angling to a drain—
also our questions. How many
bodies a week? Do they sit up?
What if a shotgun, what if a bomb?
Did he have his wife undress
the ladies? Next came the putty
and fake blood and your own choice
of face wounds, gapped open so you
could river a finger through it.
Finally, the refrigerator room
and a draped body on a gurney.
Draining them, he said, *you feel*
this energy, either good or bad.
I've buried them all—alcoholics,
pot heads, convicts. And once,
a prostitute. Spirits of men
leaked right out of her, he said.

It's a matter of accumulation,
what you take in. His voice
lifted me straight onto the table.
Razored me open. He was reaching in.
My stomach. My liver, my kidneys.
Lifting one organ at a time.
I wasn't afraid. I wanted it this easy—
the heart something you could
weigh in the palm, goodness
as simple as turning down a smoke.

Throwing Papers

My feet carved an invisible path
of shortcuts until I knew every
geranium petal and rusted croquet hoop
and how to spell fifty-two names.
I was learning the mathematics
of adulthood, how to multiply myself
for Christmas tips and divide out
reprimands. And though I grew lighter
with each paper I threw, I felt
the same sky, the same bruised infinity
pressing down. And only peeling paint
and another story problem to help me
navigate my happiness. Do I wait
to collect from Old Lady Perkins
until after she buries her husband?
Do I tell the Colonel I scratched
his restored cherry Corvair? Yes,
and no. Whatever helped balance
the month. Compensations? A sweating
can of soda maybe, and the things
I found—women's nylons tied in a bow,
then John Sousa sheet music. And once,
stepping past a swing set, a goat head.
Fleshy, one-eared, it lay in the mums,
like a dimpled work boot. I rubbed
its jaw. Tried subtracting the gristled
windpipe, the necklace of ants.
Added fur to the leathered face.
Zeroes still blanked the eye sockets,
the tongue lolling like a pointer.
Across the street, in kitchens dressed
for the latest holiday, families
were lifting careful spoonfuls
of gravy. I was doing just enough

to keep them happy, a few hours
in the cold each week, cursory hellos,
all for three-and-a-half cents per paper,
per day, per forever, collected myself.

Counting

Where are they—those mornings when counting
the bones inside a lover's hand passed
as knowledge? My shoes are black, my mouth
sour with this morning's breakfast. I have
a burn scar like one of the Great Lakes
on my neck. Those workmen in orange shirts
eating chicken under the maple do not know
my name. If the body replaces itself every
seven years, I'm halfway between my fourth
and fifth incarnations. But who can say
if I'm new above the waist or below. I've
saved numbers in my wallet that will not
save me. Is it whiteness or something else
I close my eyes on? When I open them,
a severity of bread crumbs and pigeon wings
tipped by too much sun. I'm tired of defining.

Interiors

Take the mail in, lift the watering can . . .
Each task erased me a little, until
I was nosing through the rooms on automatic,
thinking of the two daughters. Leggy
impossible girls, tennis players, already
in college. Girls who wolf-whistled
or honked if they saw me, but never meant it.
The whole family was touring Greece, and I
was here, their little brother's friend
trying to rub against their ghosts. I never
opened the windows. Never thought of it.
Which meant a thickness when I moved,
rooms nerved and borderline electric.
Every sofa and plumped chair an essay question
in breathing. And everywhere, arrows pointing
what not to touch next. I fingered blouses,
sniffed towels, buried my wrist in a jar
of orphaned buttons. When nothing brought
the girls closer, I'd give up and crank on
the radio. Trust my feet to the numbered
instructions above the sink. And at night
I floated. Their pool was oval, more murky
than clear. From the garden, the boomerang
grunts of toads, drowned ones bellying the tile.
Mostly I kept to the deep end. Rain water,
sprinkler water, water that had lipped at thighs—
that's what was holding me up. And above,
through a kaleidoscope of sycamore branches,
animals I couldn't see pinned to a wheel
of stars. I was at the center of something.
I kept the lights off to blur my edges.

Bath House Overlooking Family Cemetery

The door opens with the elastic pop
of a refrigerator at midnight, air wet
and warm like the breath of running
dogs. I know the smell—not of sickness
or boiled eggs, but of mildew eating
old boards, of leached minerals,
almost of urine, the closed-in ripeness
of sweaty relatives settling their weight
against car seats in late afternoon.
And the bubbling water—how I sink,
how I bury myself, washing my mouth
with the taste of nails and draining
caves. Below, where irises map the hill,
cows nose among toppled gravestones.
They could be eating, they could be
looking for their own kind of door.

Smoke

He'd prefer a preacher
with a gap-toothed smile
and enough moves to dribble
his way through purgatory.
I'm sitting in the last pew,
wishing coaches were canonized.
I mean the real ones,
who feel it in their thighs
when a shot goes up.
Richard Coons did.
Basketball was his blood.
He invoked the gods
in the name of trajectory
and sent us to hell
for a missed pick.

If it's respects we're paying,
we ought to reconvene
at the old gym—where kicked-in
Coke machines flank the door
and smoky shafts of light
fall from dirtied windows.
Picture altar boys in jocks
and cassocks running lay-ins,
the choir singing rockabilly,
and Richard in a sweatshirt
yelling from his box.
Afterward, we could pry up
the boards, drop him at the baseline,
ask Cousy and Havlicek
to pray him into Heaven.

I'll do my honors, later,
at the city park. Make it dusk,

or just after, street lights
flickering on, a pair of lovers
on the grass inventing new
variations on loneliness.
I'll eye the chain-link net
and start from mid court.
A head fake for passing
hoodlums, a stutter step
for Richard, then four dribbles,
a lift of my knee, and I'll
rise, rise, a slow smoke.

Against Cosmology

Almost too much—the fingers of sky,
the hill like an accusing face. I want
subtlety, the wonder of a moon looking
only like a moon, of things unfolding
slowly and meaning nothing. I want
to walk bare streets and pause beneath
an upstairs window and say, with no
conviction at all, that a laid-off mechanic
named Ignacio or Max is frying liver
by the light of his horoscope—and happily
ignoring the future. Tonight I want
to tread water, and not think of other
pools, just this one—how dead leaves
cluster in the deep end and bats swoop
on insects. I want to see shrubs
and flower stalks and cats sliding
across ragged lawns without seeing
myself. I want to stare at the stars
and say they are not worth their light
without being pulled into darkness.

Elegy for Donald Pugmire, Photographer

Working his lighting console from a chair,
he called himself Lazy Prophet, Conjurer.
With the flick of a switch, he created visions,
studio bursting into waterfall and sunset,

painted doves circling an ocean blue enough
to swim in. Then ruin, a world of ice and ink,
moons and midnight cats. When a client arrived,
he was all commotion, coaxing like a preacher,

carving air with sweeps of his hand. One woman
with crimson lips he buried in green tomatoes.
Another he armed with a blow dryer and a magazine,
then faced her off with a smiling bull moose.

He gave people versions of themselves no mirror
could duplicate, eyes wild and intimate,
mouths set whispering forgotten dialects.
They lilted out of his office on borrowed wings.

On Sundays, his studio was a drawer
he closed against everyone but himself.
Alone with his Leica and a hatful of film,
he'd brood over a sliced apple or pouty iris,

sometimes for hours, his way of wrestling disbelief,
of cracking a window into the other world.
A budding begonia could teach him regeneration;
a broken sand dollar, the terror and expediency

of the moral law. Or at least he said they could.
All I have is his camera and a few portraits,
the ones he rarely showed: oily faces
of strangers staring from the cement bowels

of the city, staring like Lazarus or Jairus's daughter.
An idiot gas attendant. A girl wrapped in curtains.
A shoe shiner wreathed in his own smoke.
Sometimes I think they're his eyes staring.

Once, mixing chemicals, his glasses almost glowing,
he told me we were falling at that moment,
at every moment, through a slow funnel of days,
that when we die the funnel opens on itself

and gobbles everything we've done, spitting out
hours minutes every increment of time, leaving
us a glove of accumulated light that we wear
forever. He only explained it once. Since then

his house has been torn down, his studio converted
into a bakery run by Laotians. It's almost morning,
and I'm sitting in Eva's, the corner booth,
where Don used to come for omelettes. He'd like

this waitress, the quiet drama of her mouth.
She serves with a stiff upper arm. If he were here,
he would look, focus, then pour himself,
like coffee, into her troubles. All I can do is tip.

And learn to trust the cool eye of a borrowed
camera. Fly specks on a dirtied window could
teach me. The stripped Chevy across the street,
sitting on blocks. Even this gaping napkin holder.

Fortune of some sort, this early hour—my hunger,
her hands, this light. Wild horses in each finger.

Cityscape

Houston, Texas

Finally, after two gutted warehouses, the railroad
tracks—telescoping lines that unzip the city. My son
pats their rust like a believer, then pulls at me. North,
because the landmarks are mangier. The bleeding

octagon house, the styrofoam plant with its drifts
of pastel pellets, the re-tread place thick with lizards
and fat raccoons. Somewhere behind us simmers
our complex—Lego apartments stacked three high

and lounging imports that chirp in Japanese if you
touch them. We rest beside the chemical depot,
in shade that smells like chlorine, only sweeter.
That's when my son starts his hoppity groin dance.

If I'm lucky I have three minutes. Forty feet
into the cottonwoods, me carrying him, I find a trail,
then a homeless camp. No, not a camp—a tree-walled
efficiency with scraps of dirty sky blowing above.

What can I say about English muffins and a dented
mannequin's head in a grocery cart? Or a mortuary
calendar nailed to a tree? Impossible, all of it,
which is why when my son starts hopping again

I first think celebration. Why not? There's sun
breaking through, and a casket and glossy dead president
for every month. And right here, firemen's boots waiting
for an angel to slide down a greased column of air.

I unsnap my son and join him at the bush. A pair
of mating dragonflies dips to the puddle, hovers. He points:
What those? Dragons, I say, making a helicopter
out of what feels good. The piss smell is hot and clean

and somehow accidental, and all around us leaves
rustle like a library read by the wind. Afterwards,
I turn the calendar forward three months to May
and a sour-looking Grover Cleveland. Rub his belly for luck.

Peach

Call it treason, but I'm eating my way
south. Chilean peaches, swaddled in green
tissue. I buy them $1.79 a pound.
In Kalamazoo, in the teeth of winter.
Tart enough they bite back. By the shape,
this one could be Allende's heart.
I palm it, I lick its seams. Each day
I feel a little more Marxist. The fuzz
part is obscene, so I peel it with my teeth.
I take a long time. Think of peaches
trundled to market on a scooter, peaches
filling a maid's mesh handbag. I once saw
a girl in a catechism dress sliver off
a piece for her brother. Her mouth to his.
I never should have quit the Peace Corps.
I happen to be dragging the wet part
slowly across my cheek. If Congress
would try this, if the President of CBS . . .
I'm ready to donate everything to La Leche
League. I'm taking my first big bite.
I wish I was mestizo and uncircumcised.
I wish I could cozy up beside those sad
Easter Island faces. I want book titles
running up the spine, not down, whirlpools
in the toilet spinning the wrong way.
It's firm, this peach flesh—with threads
of blood and history running through it.
Sometimes I think I'm a she. I want Reagan
to remember everything he never was.
Go ahead, count the letters in his name.
Ronald Wilson Reagan. 666. All the U.S.
can offer. South is always better.
Chickens in bed with you, a llama watchdog.
I'm dribbling peach juice and learning

to disembowel with a toothbrush. I wish
San Martín could heal in English, that penguins
would teach me how to carry eggs. I'm
investing in copper futures and madly
trilling my r's. On my taxes I claim
children named María de la Purísima and Jesús.
And now I'm down to the pit, which I'm
biting. An entire hemisphere in my mouth,
Pablo Neruda between my teeth. I'm listening
with the ear of a Mapuche Indian. Closing
my eyes to speak. *Hetcha batgutcha sitza.*
Rough translation: eat bat guano, America.
All made up, I admit. But I *want* their talk.
I *want* those tough SOBs on my side. I blow
my nose and whole soccer teams fly out.
I will show this to every kind of doctor.
I wish Gabriela Mistral had nursed me.
When I marry, it will be for exquisite
black eyebrows and wide hips. When I
conceive, I'll burn white, then red,
then redder. This peach sweet as seven Edens
and a peasant virgin. Sweet as Chilean
cowboys. Already, it's churning inside me.

Driving I-70

Late August, windows down, alpine highway
unwinding under a plush, do-nothing sky.
For company, there's a DJ from Cheyenne
with the stoutness of God in his voice.
Listen long enough and each fencepost starts
looking like a radiant Mary. Then flames bloom,
cartoonish and impossible, in the rear-view—
your hammered-together trailer on fire.
First thing: pull over and unhook. Call it
a test case, only everything burning is yours.
Work shirts letting go of their stitches,
letters turning to petroglyphs of ash. Try dirt,
or maybe a hunter's jacket. And if in a slurry
of motion, the afternoon tilts, then slides
away, let it go. Ignore the tattooed trucker
running with a shovel, the extinguishers
and water jugs, the shimmer of voices squawking
How in Hell's name? and *Mercy, mercy.* Wait
for quiet, steam lifting on a broken breeze.
Then look it over—burnt towels and bedding,
pants shorn off at the knee, the melted ganglia
of neckties. Inhale. Is it loss you smell,
or your body's salt burned into something darker
and more pure? Take a few steps. Think of rivers.
Follow the delicate ash drifting over fences
and fields, over a dazed cluster of Holsteins
chewing again what they've already swallowed.

Photo by Veryl Larsen

Lance Larsen (Ph.D., University of Houston) is poetry editor of *Literature and Belief*. His poems have appeared in *Paris Review*, *Shenandoah*, *Hudson Review*, *Kenyon Review* and else-where, and he has received awards from the Cultural Arts Council of Houston and the Utah Arts Council. He teaches at Brigham Young University and is married to Jacqui Biggs Larsen, a mixed media artist. They have three children.

Richard Howard has published ten books of poems and received numerous awards, including the Pulitzer Prize and a MacArthur Fellowship. A distinguished translator of French literature, he has been awarded the P.E.N. Translation Medal and the American Book Award. An expanded version of his collection of essays, *Alone with America: Essays on the Art of Poetry in the United States*, was reissued in 1980. He is a chancellor of the Academy of American Poets and teaches at Columbia.